UNLOCKING THE
PROPHETIC
MYSTERIES
OF ISRAEL

STUDY GUIDE

UNLOCKING THE
PROPHETIC
MYSTERIES
OF ISRAEL

STUDY GUIDE

JONATHAN BERNIS

**CHARISMA
HOUSE**

Most CHARISMA HOUSE BOOK GROUP products are available at special quantity discounts for bulk purchase for sales promotions, premiums, fund-raising, and educational needs. For details, write Charisma House Book Group, 600 Rinehart Road, Lake Mary, Florida 32746, or telephone (407) 333-0600.

UNLOCKING THE PROPHETIC MYSTERIES OF ISRAEL STUDY GUIDE by Jonathan Bernis
Published by Charisma House
Charisma Media/Charisma House Book Group
600 Rinehart Road
Lake Mary, Florida 32746
www.charismahouse.com

This book or parts thereof may not be reproduced in any form, stored in a retrieval system, or transmitted in any form by any means—electronic, mechanical, photocopy, recording, or otherwise—without prior written permission of the publisher, except as provided by United States of America copyright law.

Unless otherwise noted, all Scripture quotations are from the Tree of Life Version. Copyright © 2015 by the Messianic Jewish Family Bible Society. Used by permission of the Messianic Jewish Family Bible Society.

Scripture quotations marked NIV are taken from the Holy Bible, New International Version®, NIV®. Copyright © 1973, 1978, 1984, 2011 by Biblica, Inc.™ Used by permission of Zondervan. All rights reserved worldwide. www.zondervan.com. The "NIV" and "New International Version" are trademarks registered in the United States Patent and Trademark Office by Biblica, Inc.™

Scripture quotations marked NKJV are taken from the New King James Version®. Copyright © 1982 by Thomas Nelson. Used by permission. All rights reserved.

Copyright © 2017 by Jonathan Bernis
All rights reserved

Cover design by Justin Evans

Visit the author's website at www.jewishvoice.org.

International Standard Book Number: 978-1-62999-517-5

While the author has made every effort to provide accurate telephone numbers and Internet addresses at the time of publication, neither the publisher nor the author assumes any responsibility for errors or for changes that occur after publication.

18 19 20 21 22 — 7 6 5 4 3 2
Printed in the United States of America

CONTENTS

INTRODUCTION

ARE WE LIVING in the last days? All around the world people—even those who don't think of themselves as religious—are getting the sense that we're headed toward the end. Radical jihadists are unleashing their terror on peaceful city streets, killing teenagers at a concert and children celebrating Bastille Day in France. Racial tensions are escalating in the United States as Russia renews efforts to expand its control. We'd like to think the world is becoming a better place, but the truth is we are the same old flawed humanity we have always been.

The Bible tells us that in the last days "hard times will come—for people will be lovers of self, lovers of money, boastful, arrogant, blasphemers, disobedient to parents, ungrateful, unholy, hardhearted, unforgiving, backbiting, without self-control, brutal, hating what is good, treacherous, reckless, conceited, lovers of pleasure rather than lovers of God, holding to an outward form of godliness but denying its power" (2 Tim. 3:1–5).

That passage paints a vivid picture of our world today! Yes, the end of the age is near, but that is not a bad thing for those who belong to God and serve Him diligently. The end does not mean destruction for God's people but rather redemption and the emergence of a new chapter of history, one of peace and freedom from suffering. Despite the terrors we see all around us, God is still in control, and He has a plan to bring everything together for our good. As Yeshua (Jesus) Himself said, "Now when these things begin to happen, stand straight and lift up your heads, because your salvation is near!" (Luke 21:28).

At the Center of It All

At the center of these end-time events is the tiny nation of Israel. Make no mistake, if you want to understand what God is doing in these last days, you must understand what He is doing with Israel. In this study guide you will explore seven keys to understanding Israel's past, present, and future role in God's plan to recover a corrupt and lost world. His plan will culminate in the utter defeat of evil and all principalities and powers, and the establishment of a Messianic age of peace and prosperity. And you can be part of it. By digging deep into these seven keys, you can begin to understand not only end-times prophecy and the signs of the times but also the role all believers play in the return of our Messiah and Savior, Yeshua.

This study guide consists of four sessions designed for individual or group study. It is meant to be used in tandem with *Unlocking the Prophetic Mysteries of Israel*, as each session includes questions drawn from the book for you to ponder or discuss, along with relevant Scripture. At the end of each session you will be encouraged to consider ways you can bless Israel and to pray for the peace of Jerusalem and salvation of the Jewish people.

Take your time as you work through the material. Carefully consider each question, and devote some time each day to praying for Israel and the Jewish people. My prayer is that as you come to understand the truths within these pages and share them with others, you will be salt and light to a church that for the most part does not understand how Israel ties in to their salvation and the future redemption of the world.

Just as the Jewish people are experiencing a partial blindness that keeps them from recognizing Yeshua as Messiah, much of the church is walking in a partial blindness that keeps them from recognizing the role of Israel in God's plan for the redemption of the nations. But the better you understand these prophetic mysteries, the more that will change.

How to Use This Study Guide

Individual study
Unlocking the Prophetic Mysteries of Israel Study Guide is made for individual reading and use. Here are some simple steps for getting the most out of it:

- Read the related chapters in *Unlocking the Prophetic Mysteries of Israel.*

- Answer questions in each session, exploring the scriptures as you do.

- Use the journal to record any insights, scriptures, prayer requests, or answers to prayer you receive as you pray daily for Israel and the Jewish people.

Bible studies and small groups

Unlocking the Prophetic Mysteries of Israel Study Guide is also made for use in Bible studies and small groups. Here are some simple steps for the one leading the group:

- Have participants first read *Unlocking the Prophetic Mysteries of Israel* and obtain a copy of the study guide so they can fully participate, explore, fill in the answers, and complete the applications for each week.

- Prepare weekly teachings based on the chapters and scriptures in this study guide (5–20 minutes).

- Lead the group in a discussion based on the questions in each session.

- Suggest that participants look for ways to bless Israel in the coming week through prayer, evangelism, activism, or financial support of a ministry that seeks to bless the Jewish people.

- Close the study with a time of prayer. Assign next week's reading assignment in preparation for the upcoming class.

Whether you use this guide individually or in a small group, it will help equip you to understand Israel's role—and yours—in the end times. Today we are witnessing things that the prophets of Israel longed to see. God is fulfilling His Word in our generation! Unlock a greater knowledge about the last days by understanding these seven crucial keys…and discover the crucial responsibility each believer has regarding God's chosen people.

SESSION ONE

WHY ISRAEL?

KEY ONE:
THE SEED PROMISE

Before you begin, read the introduction and chapter 1 of *Unlocking the Prophetic Mysteries of Israel.*

ISRAEL IS A tiny nation spread over a few thousand square miles of desert and hills in the Middle East. It is only slightly larger than the state of New Jersey, and it is certainly not the world's richest or most powerful nation. Yet to God it is the most important nation on Earth—the Bible tells us that Israel is the apple of God's eye. In this first session we will discover why the history and future of this planet are so intricately tied to Israel and what it is about Israel's destiny that causes Satan to have such a deep hatred for the Jewish people.

WHY ISRAEL?

Israel is and always has been central in God's redemptive plan for mankind. God's Son, Yeshua (Jesus) of Nazareth, gave His life for our sins in Jerusalem nearly two thousand years ago. It was there that He was crucified and buried, rose from the dead, and then ascended into heaven. God chose to have His temple built in Jerusalem and to dwell there among His people. It was in Israel that He performed great signs and wonders. And Israel is where Yeshua will ultimately return to, fulfilling prophecies written thousands of years ago.

The introduction to *Unlocking the Prophetic Mysteries of Israel* lists three reasons Israel plays such an important role in God's end-times plan. Look up the

3

following passages, and use them to explain why this tiny nation is so important to end-times events.

- Ezekiel 34:11–13 and Isaiah 11:10–12:

_____

_____

_____

_____

_____

_____

- Joel 2:25–27 (Tree of Life), or Joel 2:27–32 (other translations):

_____

_____

_____

_____

_____

_____

_____

- Zechariah 12:10:

_____

_____

_____

_____

_____

_____

_____

In the last days God will regather His people to Israel, and He will pour out His Spirit upon the Jewish people—and these things are happening now, right before our eyes. The Jewish people are returning to their homeland after being scattered to nations around the world, and Jewish people are coming to faith in Yeshua in record numbers. In fact, it's been said that more Jewish people have come to know Yeshua in the last forty years than in the previous nineteen hundred years.

We are living in exciting times. Things the ancient prophets of Israel longed to see are being fulfilled before our eyes. God is bringing about the final wrap-up of history, and He has honored us by allowing us to be part of it. Yet we must be careful not to believe everything we hear about Israel and the end times.

How can you discern truth from fiction about the end-times events relating to Israel?

_____

_____

_____

_____

_____

_____

_____

Can we know the date of Messiah's return?

_____

_____

_____

_____

_____

_____

What does Matthew 24:42–44 tell us about how we must await Yeshua's return?

_____

_____

_____

_____

_____

_____

Bible prophecies are being fulfilled all around us, but the study of prophecy is fertile ground for false teachers and charlatans. Sadly there is a great deal of inaccuracy and sensationalism mixed in with the truth. But we must not throw the baby out with the bathwater. We must be like the Bereans, who "search[ed] the Scriptures each day to see whether these things were true" (Acts 17:11).

THE COMING MESSIAH

Some people get confused by what the Scriptures say about the coming Messiah. In some passages He is presented as a great conqueror who will wage war on His enemies. In others He is presented as a meek and humble servant who would be rejected, suffer, and die. The ancient sages of Israel thought there were two Messiahs, one who would be rejected as Joseph was and one who would restore Israel's golden age and rule over a thriving kingdom as King David did.

> **Describe what Isaiah 53:1–7 and Revelation 19:11–16 say about the Messiah. How can the Messiah be both a great conqueror of His enemies and a meek and humble servant?**

_____

_____

_____

_____

_____

_____

_____

We can be sure that the Messiah is coming again as the great King of kings and Lord of lords. He will vanquish evil and rule over all nations. But until the Messiah comes, Satan will continue to do anything in his power to destroy the Jewish people. Why? It's because of the first key to unlocking the prophetic mysteries of Israel—the seed promise.

KEY ONE:
THE SEED PROMISE

We've all seen the horrific pictures of Holocaust survivors—emaciated men, women, and children who seem to be only days away from death by starvation. They look out at the world through sunken, lifeless eyes that have seen unbelievable horror.

It defies belief that six million people died in Nazi extermination camps simply because they were Jewish. It is difficult to understand, much less explain, how human beings could commit such unspeakable abuse and torture. It only makes sense when you realize there was a supernatural aspect to the level of hatred directed toward the Jewish people.

Satan hates the Jewish people with a passion, and he does so because he knows something most believers don't—that God's plan to redeem this world comes through the Jewish people. Our redemption—our victory—is the enemy's defeat. And as the time for our victory comes closer, he is becoming increasingly determined in his effort to destroy the Jewish people.

DIG DEEP INTO
THE SCRIPTURES

Read Genesis 3:15; 4:1; 12:2–3.

Define *protoevangelium*.

_____

_____

_____

_____

_____

_____

_____

How does Genesis 3:15 prophesy of a coming redeemer?

_____

_____

_____

_____

_____

_____

_____

How do we know from Genesis 3:15 that Yeshua would be born of a virgin?

_____

_____

_____

_____

_____

What does Genesis 3:15 reveal about why Satan hates the Jewish people so deeply?

_____

_____

_____

_____

_____

What insight does Genesis 3:15 give about the suffering of the Jewish people throughout history?

_____

_____

_____

_____

_____

_____

_____

What does Genesis 4:1 reveal about who Adam and Eve thought the promised redeemer was?

_____

_____

_____

_____

_____

What does Genesis 12:2–3 reveal about the "seed promise"?

_____

_____

_____

_____

_____

_____

A death sentence has been decreed over Satan, and it will come to pass. Satan has attempted to destroy the children of Abraham throughout history. But the evil one's efforts will fail. The Messiah will come again and vanquish His enemy.

Unmasking Hate

The devil didn't make the Nazis carry out Hitler's demonic scheme. They chose to side with evil and perpetrate genocide on the Jewish people. Sadly, even knowledge of the Scriptures didn't prevent Nazis and many Christians through the centuries from justifying their hatred of the Jews.

What are some ways Nazis and Christians justified their hatred of the Jewish people?

_____

_____

_____

_____

_____

_____

What are some negative stereotypes you've heard about the Jewish people? How do you respond when you hear such statements?

_____

_____

_____

_____

_____

_____

_____

Explain whom Yeshua was referring to in John 8:44: "You are of your father the devil, and you want to do the desires of your father. He was a murderer from the beginning and does not stand in the truth, because there is no truth in him. Whenever he speaks lies he is just being himself—for he is a liar and the father of lies."

_____

_____

_____

_____

_____

_____

What do the following passages of Scripture tell us about how Yeshua feels about the Jewish people?

- Matthew 10:5–6:

_____

_____

13

_____

_____

_____

_____

_____

- Matthew 15:21–28:

_____

_____

_____

_____

_____

- Luke 19:41:

_____

_____

_____

_____

_____

How has the book *The Protocols of the Elders of Zion* been used to perpetuate false beliefs about the Jewish people and instigate violence toward them?

_____

_____

_____

_____

_____

_____

How did Martin Luther's writings help convince Hitler and the Nazis they were doing "God's work" when they committed genocide against the Jewish people?

_____

_____

_____

_____

_____

_____

Is violence against the Jewish people a thing of the past? Has the situation improved since World War II?

_____

_____

_____

_____

_____

_____

_____

How did God preserve the Jewish people each of the following times when Satan tried to destroy them?

• During the Israelites' enslavement in Egypt:

_____

_____

_____

_____

_____

_____

• At the time of Haman's attempt at genocide:

_____

_____

_____

_____

_____

- During Herod's murder of Israelite baby boys:

_____

_____

_____

_____

_____

_____

- At Yeshua's false arrest and crucifixion:

_____

_____

_____

_____

_____

What significant redemptive act of God occurred after each of the following events?

- Pharaoh's enslaving of the children of Israel:

_____

_____

_____

_____

_____

_____

_____

- Herod's rise to power:

_____

_____

_____

_____

_____

- The emergence of Adolf Hitler:

_____

_____

_____

_____

_____

What does Jeremiah 31:34–36 tell us about why Satan has been unable to eradicate the Jewish people?

_____

_____

_____

_____

_____

_____

Satan knows his time is short, and he is doing every-thing within his power to keep our Messiah from returning. He is like a panicked snake trapped in a corner, striking out in all directions to inflict as much damage as he can to escape the judgment that has been pronounced against him. But we already know how the story ends: "And the devil who deceived them was thrown into the lake of fire and brimstone, where the beast and the false prophet are too, and they shall be tortured day and night forever and ever" (Rev. 20:10).

BLESS ISRAEL

The devil loves it when we refuse to see people as indi-viduals created in the image of God but instead see them as merely members of a larger group we don't like. It is unlikely the Nazis ever thought about the fact that they were killing fathers and mothers, sons and daughters, hus-bands and wives. As far as they were concerned, they were killing Jews as an undesirable group, not individuals.

Yale University historian Jaroslav Pelikan posed a salient question when he asked: "Would there have been such anti-Semitism, would there have been so many pogroms [orga-nized massacres], would there have been an Auschwitz, if every Christian church and every Christian home had focused its devotion and icons of Mary not only as Mother of God and Queen of heaven but as the Jewish maiden and the new Miriam, and on icons of Christ not only as a Pantocrator but as *Rabbi Jeshua bar-Joseph*, Rabbi Jesus of Nazareth?"[1]

Why do you think so many contemporary representations of Yeshua still depict a northern European surrounded by others of the same descent?

_____

_____

_____

_____

_____

_____

_____

_____

_____

_____

_____

_____

_____

_____

PRAYER JOURNAL

Use this space to record any insights, scriptures, or answers to prayer you receive as you spend time praying for the peace of Jerusalem and the salvation of the Jewish people.

_____

_____

_____

_____

_____

_____

_____

_____

_____

_____

_____

_____

_____

_____

_____

_____

_____

_____

SESSION TWO

KEY TWO:
The Abrahamic Blessing

KEY THREE:
The New Covenant

Before you begin, read chapters 2 and 3 of
Unlocking the Prophetic Mysteries of Israel.

NOW THAT WE know why Israel is so important in end-times events and why Satan is so set on destroying the Jewish people, we can explore the next two keys to unlocking the prophetic mysteries of Israel. Not only are these keys critical to our understanding of Israel's role in the last days, but they will also help us appreciate the incredible gift that has been given to every follower of Yeshua, both Jew and Gentile, through the Jewish people.

KEY TWO:
THE ABRAHAMIC BLESSING

Abraham was a man of great faith—he had to be. Just think about how God told him to leave his land, his relatives, and his father's house to go to a land God would show him. Even if the technology had existed, a GPS would have done him no good because he had no destination to input.

Has God ever led you to step out into the unknown where you had to walk by faith, not knowing where He was leading you? If so, describe your experience.

_____

_____

_____

_____

_____

_____

Abraham didn't know where he was headed when he set off from his homeland. But he had a word from God and a promise:

> My heart's desire is to make you into a great nation, to bless you, to make your name great so that you may be a blessing. My desire is to bless those who bless you, but whoever curses you I will curse, and in you all the families of the earth will be blessed.
> —Genesis 12:2–3

Within that passage of Scripture is the second key to unlocking the prophetic mysteries of Israel—understanding that God has pronounced an eternal blessing upon the children of Israel and He has not rescinded it. Those who bless the Jewish people will be blessed. Those who curse them will be cursed. It's as simple as that.

Consider the following passages of Scripture. Describe how God responded to those who blessed Israel and to those who cursed His people.

- 2 Chronicles 20:

_____

_____

_____

_____

_____

_____

_____

- 2 Kings 19:

_____

_____

_____

_____

_____

_____

- Joshua 10:1–14:

_____

_____

_____

_____

_____

_____

Share some modern examples from chapter 2 of *Unlocking the Prophetic Mysteries of Israel* of how nations that have cursed Israel have been cursed and those that have blessed Israel have been blessed.

_____

_____

_____

_____

_____

_____

Do you believe America's future prosperity is connected to how it treats Israel? Explain.

_____

_____

_____

_____

_____

Does supporting Israel mean we support everything the nation does? Explain.

_____

_____

_____

_____

_____

_____

THE LAND OF ISRAEL

One of the most contentious political issues related to Israel is the nation's right to the land.

Do you believe that God gave Abraham and his descendants the right to the land that is today the modern State of Israel? Explain.

_____

_____

_____

_____

_____

_____

What do the following passages of Scripture reveal about the right of the Jewish people to inhabit the land of Israel?

• Genesis 13:14–17:

_____

_____

- Exodus 32:13:

- 2 Chronicles 20:7:

Does the fact that Israel is the apple of God's eye mean He loves other nations less? Consider Acts 10:34–35.

_____

_____

_____

_____

_____

How have the Jewish people been a blessing to the world, both spiritually and practically?

_____

_____

_____

_____

_____

_____

The principle of divine blessing and cursing based on how nations and individuals treat the Jewish people is still in effect. How we align ourselves with this decree will determine whether God blesses us. You can be blessed by being a conduit of blessing to the Jewish people. And the greatest blessing you can give the Jewish people is the gospel. Not only would you be introducing them to their Messiah; you would also be leading them to experience the blessings of the new covenant, which is the third key to unlocking the prophetic mysteries of Israel.

KEY THREE:
THE NEW COVENANT

The prophet Jeremiah declared: "'Behold, days are coming'—it is a declaration of Adonai—'when I will make a new covenant with the house of Israel and with the house of Judah...I will put My Torah within them. Yes, I will write it on their heart. I will be their God and they will be My people'" (Jer. 31:30, 32).

Jeremiah spoke those words during a very difficult time in Israel's history. The kingdom had been split in two. The northern kingdom of Israel had been overrun by the Assyrians in 722 BC. Then, a century and a half later, the southern kingdom of Judah was defeated by the Babylonians. Jerusalem lay in ruins, and the temple was destroyed. Most of the population was in captivity in Babylon.

But at no time had God forsaken or forgotten His people. He spoke through Jeremiah to declare that a day was coming when the children of Israel would be forgiven and restored as a nation—when God would establish a new covenant through which He would relate to His people in a new and intimate way.

What is replacement theology, and how is it at odds with God's message in Jeremiah 31:30–33?

_____

_____

_____

_____

_____

_____

_____

How can those who are not Jewish by birth partake in this new covenant?

_____

_____

_____

_____

_____

_____

What are the four key aspects of the new covenant? Why are they so important to understand?

_____

_____

_____

_____

_____

_____

_____

_____

What does John 1:12 reveal about the kind of relationship God wants to have with us?

_____

_____

_____

_____

_____

_____

DIG DEEP INTO THE SCRIPTURES

Read Jeremiah 31:33.

Where does this passage say the law is written?

_____

_____

_____

_____

_____

_____

How does this contrast with Mosaic Law?

_____

_____

_____

_____

_____

_____

Have you experienced a time when "the law" became personal to you, when the motivation to do what is right came from the inside and not external rules? If so, describe.

_____

_____

_____

_____

_____

_____

The Mosaic covenant rests on our shoulders like a heavy mantle, with assorted rules and laws we can never fully keep.

Although we may attempt to do so with great diligence, it is simply impossible. In the Book of Galatians, Paul says we are no longer under the law. Some teachers claim this means the law has disappeared and no longer exists, but that is inaccurate. Rather, the law has been taken off tablets of stone and parchment and inscribed on our hearts. And because of this we have been given the power to be "doers of the word" (James 1:22) through the indwelling of the Holy Spirit.

ALL ISRAEL SHALL BE SAVED

Looking again at Jeremiah 31:33, we read that God declared, "No longer will each teach his neighbor or each his brother, saying: 'Know Adonai,' for they will all know Me, from the least of them to the greatest." This verse refers to a time in history when either all or the vast majority of the Jewish people will know their God intimately.

The apostle Paul expounded on this promise, revealing some reasons we have not yet seen this come to pass:

> For I do not desire, brethren, that you should be ignorant of this mystery, lest you should be wise in your own opinion, that blindness in part has happened to Israel until the fullness of the Gentiles has come in. And so all Israel will be saved, as it is written: "The Deliverer will come out of Zion, and He will turn away ungodliness from Jacob; for this is My covenant with them, when I take away their sins."
> —ROMANS 11:25–27, NKJV

Romans 11 indicates that one reason this promise hasn't manifested yet is because the Jewish people are experiencing a spiritual blindness. Does this mean God struck the Jews with this blindness? Explain.

_____

_____

_____

_____

_____

_____

Has there ever been a time when there were no Jewish believers in Messiah? Explain.

_____

_____

_____

_____

_____

How have Jewish believers in Yeshua often been treated after they came to faith in Messiah?

_____

_____

_____

_____

_____

_____

What does Zechariah 12:10 reveal about how long this spiritual blindness will remain over the Jewish people?

_____

_____

_____

_____

_____

_____

What is the time referred to as "the fullness of the Gentiles" in Romans 11:25?

_____

_____

_____

_____

_____

_____

How is the church also blind?

_____

_____

_____

_____

_____

THE POWER OF FORGIVENESS

One final aspect of the new covenant that is important to understand is that God will forgive the sins of those who come into this covenant with Him. And not only will He forgive them, but He will also forget those sins completely, as Jeremiah 31:33 says: "For I will forgive their iniquity, their sin I will remember no more."

How does forgiveness of sins under the new covenant stand in contrast to forgiveness under the Mosaic covenant?

_____

_____

_____

_____

_____

What does 2 Corinthians 5:17 say is the only thing that can wash our sins away and make us completely clean?

_____

_____

_____

_____

_____

_____

What does the story of the prodigal son teach us about the Father's willingness to forgive?

_____

_____

_____

_____

_____

_____

_____

It is, perhaps, understandably difficult to forgive terrorists such as ISIS or those who perpetrated the horrors of the Holocaust. But Yeshua tells us to pray for our enemies. Whom do you have a hard time forgiving, and why?

_____

_____

_____

_____

_____

_____

_____

Understanding God's new covenant with His chosen people and His commitment to fulfill this covenant is a highly important key to understanding God's end-times plan. And that plan involves you because in these last days we can expect to see the blindness coming off of the eyes of the Jewish people in greater and greater numbers, as Sharon Allen's testimony illustrates.

At the end of chapter 3 we read about how Sharon Allen came to embrace Yeshua as her Messiah. What convinced you that Yeshua was the Messiah of Israel? What can you do to help Jewish people come to faith in Yeshua?

_____

_____

_____

_____

_____

_____

_____

_____

_____

_____

BLESS ISRAEL

Just as nations that bless Israel will, in turn, be blessed, the same is true of individuals, as the story of Ram from Burkina Faso shows. Every year, Ram would send a special gift to bless Messianic believers in Israel—first four dollars, then six dollars the next year, then eight dollars, and then twelve dollars. A few years back Ram traveled to Phoenix and appeared on _Jewish Voice With Jonathan Bernis_. Shortly before his visit Ram had been in Israel, where he dropped off a gift of $28,000 to help struggling Jewish families. This represented a tithe from the one hundred churches he has planted throughout Burkina Faso. Those churches now have a combined membership of over one hundred thousand people—this in a country where the majority of the population is Muslim and fewer than 25 percent of the people consider themselves Christians.

Consider the following ways you can bless Israel. Ponder or discuss the area in which you feel most called to show your support for the Jewish people.

- Stand up for the Jewish people by urging government officials to support Israel.

- Speak out against the Boycott, Divestment and Sanctions (BDS) movement, which can damage Israel economically.

- Pray daily for Jewish friends, neighbors, and coworkers.

- Pray daily for the peace of Jerusalem.

- Share the gospel with the Jewish people.

Prayer Journal

Use this space to record any insights, scriptures, or answers to prayer you receive as you spend time praying for the peace of Jerusalem and the salvation of the Jewish people.

SESSION THREE

KEY FOUR:
THE RESTORATION OF JERUSALEM

KEY FIVE:
THE GOSPEL TO THE JEW FIRST

Before you begin, read chapters 4 and 5 of
Unlocking the Prophetic Mysteries of Israel.

I N THIS SESSION we will look at an exciting sign of the end times—that in our generation, for the first time in nearly two thousand years, Jerusalem is back in Jewish hands, fulfilling the "times of the Gentiles" Yeshua prophesied in Luke 21:24. We will also discover why the gospel is to the Jew first and how that presents all Gentile believers with an essential mandate.

KEY FOUR:
THE RESTORATION OF JERUSALEM

Jerusalem is all of 48.3 square miles and of little significance compared with other commercial and industrial cities. Yet 48.3 square miles of earth has remained important in the hearts and minds of millions of people for thousands of years for one reason and one reason only: Jerusalem is important to God.

The story of Jerusalem is not just about brick and mortar that has been conquered, destroyed, and restored. It's a narrative about a people, a chosen people, tied to a chosen land with a chosen capital. It is eternal. Jerusalem does not just exist in time and space; it is also a spiritual reality. And we are told in Scripture that one day a new Jerusalem will come down from heaven adorned as a bride for her husband (Rev. 21:2).

Jerusalem is the nexus in the interaction between God and man, and it is instrumental in the fulfillment of His divine plan. It is intricately intertwined with both the history and destiny of the people of Israel. As such, it is also the focus of Satan's attack against God and his envy and hatred for God's chosen people.

Yet the fourth key to understanding Israel's role in God's end-times plan is recognizing that there is a coming restoration of Jerusalem, God's eternal capital city and the prophesied location of the Messiah's return.

After Jerusalem was destroyed in AD 70, the city was downtrodden by nation after conquering nation. Below, match the Gentile nations that occupied Jerusalem to the appropriate time frame:[1]

70–324	British
324–638	Muslims under Saladin
638–1099	Romans
1099–1187	Muslims under the Mamluks
1187–1259	Byzantines
1259–1516	Muslims
1516–1917	Ottoman Turks
1917–1948	Crusaders

Israel's victory in what war brought Jerusalem back under the control of the Jewish people after almost two thousand years?

_____

_____

_____

_____

_____

What does understanding the origins of Babylon, the anti-Jerusalem, reveal about Jerusalem?

_____

_____

_____

_____

How did Saint Augustine describe the two visions of Jerusalem in his book *City of God*?

_____

_____

_____

_____

_____

_____

Why will the City of Man always be at war with the City of God?

_____

_____

_____

_____

_____

_____

How is Abraham connected to Jerusalem? What did the city of Salem, the place where God led Abraham, become?

_____

_____

_____

_____

_____

_____

Why did God change Abram's name to Abraham when he entered Salem?

_____

_____

_____

_____

_____

_____

_____

What does Galatians 3:6–9 reveal about how Gentile believers are linked to the Jewish people?

_____

_____

_____

_____

_____

_____

How are Gentile believers and the Jewish people linked to Jerusalem?

_____

_____

_____

_____

_____

_____

_____

How did Yeshua translate Jerusalem from a temporal to a spiritual reality?

_____

_____

_____

_____

_____

_____

What composes the spiritual Jerusalem?

_____

_____

_____

_____

_____

_____

How do each of the following passages of Scripture support the premise that Jerusalem is both a temporal and a spiritual reality?

- 1 Peter 2:4–5:

_____

_____

_____

_____

_____

- 1 Corinthians 6:19:

_____

_____

_____

_____

- Ephesians 2:17–22:

_____

_____

_____

It seems God desires to fulfill His plan for both the church and the Jewish people along parallel paths. Believers and observant Jews are expecting the coming of the Messiah. One is waiting for His return to complete the work of redemption that began at Calvary; the other is anticipating the coming of King Messiah to establish a Messianic age of peace and prosperity. What many don't understand, however, is that both are waiting for the same Person—and we will all behold Him soon!

THE TIMES OF
THE GENTILES

In AD 70 the entire city of Jerusalem was destroyed, along with the temple. The Jews who were not killed either were sold into slavery or fled the city. Approximately sixty years after the temple's destruction the remaining Jewish people in what was now called Palestine (renamed by the Romans) waged another revolt against Rome. But Israel was overwhelmed, and once again the Jews were scattered throughout the region and beyond in a diaspora (dispersion). This continued for almost two thousand years until the establishment of the State of Israel in 1948.[2] Today more than 50 percent of Jewish people still live outside of the land of Israel.[3]

Centuries of persecution against Jewish people followed the Roman destruction of the temple. Scattered in all directions from their homeland, the refugees carried Jerusalem in their hearts as they wandered throughout the world—to Europe, Asia, and Africa, and eventually North and South America.

Those who stayed in the Middle East were conquered by a series of invaders, including Muslims and the Crusaders. Refugees who made their way to Europe and Asia suffered unimaginable indignities and worse, including pogroms in Russia and Eastern Europe. By 1844 there were only a few thousand Jewish people left in what was called Palestine.

Who is considered the father of the modern Zionist movement? What spurred him to action?

_____

_____

_____

_____

_____

_____

What nations were suggested by some for the new home of the Jewish state?

_____

_____

_____

_____

_____

_____

_____

_____

What likely motivated British Foreign Secretary Arthur Balfour to support the establishment of a Jewish state?

_____

_____

_____

_____

_____

How did the Six-Day War mark the fulfillment of Yeshua's revelation in Luke 21:24?

_____

_____

_____

_____

_____

Why is it significant that the "times of the Gentiles" are drawing to a close?

_____

_____

_____

_____

_____

_____

In addition to the fulfillment of the times of the Gentiles, what are some other "signs of the times"? (See Matthew 24.)

_____

_____

_____

_____

_____

_____

Ever since Yeshua ascended into heaven, people have looked at the signs of the times listed in Matthew 24 and believed the end may be near. These signs have been evident throughout history, but only now has a generation seen the restoration of Jerusalem, after almost twenty centuries— and that is significant.

Despite Satan's best efforts, Israel has been restored as a nation, and Jerusalem, as her capital. And millions of Jewish families that were scattered to the four corners of the earth have now returned to their homeland and are building new lives there. The God who brought the children of Israel out of Egypt has gathered His chosen people from the nations of the world and brought them back to the land of their fathers.

REBUILDING THE TEMPLE

The third rebuilding of the temple is a matter of great debate among end-times teachers. Some are convinced the temple will be rebuilt before Messiah returns, while others are equally convinced that the temple will be rebuilt after His coming.

A rebuilt temple is possible because the ninth chapter of Daniel talks about the abomination of desolation being set up in the temple, and Yeshua mentions this same event in Matthew 24:

> So when you see "the abomination of desolation," which was spoken of through Daniel the prophet, standing in the Holy Place (let the reader understand), then those in Judea must flee to the mountains. The one on the roof must not go down to take what is in his house, and the one in the field must not turn back to get his coat. Woe to those who are pregnant and to those who are nursing babies in those days! Pray that your escape will not happen in winter,

or on *Shabbat*. For then there will be great trouble,
such as has not happened since the beginning of the
world until now, nor ever will.

—MATTHEW 24:15–21

Although this did happen in 167 BC when the holy of
holies was desecrated by the king of the Seleucid Empire,
Antiochus IV Epiphanes, many believe it will be repeated
by the Antichrist before the return of Jesus. If this is the
case, the temple can't be desecrated again if it doesn't exist.
In other words, in this scenario the temple must be rebuilt.
And because the temple site was divinely appointed, it must
be built on its original site.

**What two structures currently sit on the location of
the Temple Mount?**

_____

_____

_____

_____

_____

_____

_____

**Describe the efforts under way to rebuild the temple,
noted in chapter 4.**

_____

_____

_____

_____

_____

_____

_____

How does the account of the valley of dry bones in Ezekiel 37 foretell the restoration of Jerusalem?

_____

_____

_____

_____

What does Revelation 21 reveal about the New Jerusalem that will exist when God establishes a new heaven and a new Earth in which all things will be restored to the way God intended them to be?

_____

_____

_____

_____

The restored Jerusalem will be a radiant, magnificent place. Zechariah 14:16 says it will be a gathering place for all the nations that will worship there during the Feast of Tabernacles: "Then all the survivors from all the nations that attacked Jerusalem will go up from year to year to worship the King, *Adonai-Tzva'ot*, and to celebrate *Sukkot*."

With the restoration of Israel in 1948 and Jerusalem reestablished as her capital and brought back under the control of the Jewish people, the times of the Gentiles are drawing to a close. These are clear signals of the end of the age. And while we cannot predict the exact time Yeshua will return, these events let us know the time is drawing near, as does the fifth key—the spread of the gospel among the Jewish people.

KEY FIVE:
THE GOSPEL TO THE JEW FIRST

You may be familiar with the story of Yeshua's encounter with the Samaritan woman at the well. Yeshua told her things about her life that a stranger would not have known, and He gave her the living water that would forever quench her thirst. There is much to glean from this account, in John chapter 4, but in discussing the fifth key, we will focus on five words Yeshua spoke during His conversation with the Samaritan woman: "Salvation is from the Jews" (John 4:22).

From the very first time He spoke to Abraham, God had already chosen Abraham's descendants to be a light to the nations and bring blessing and salvation to the world. But salvation was to be offered to them first and then through them to all the nations of the world.

The world owes the Jewish people a great debt of gratitude. Yeshua came into the world through the Jews, and they will also play a key role in His return.

To whom did Jesus preach during His earthly ministry?

_____

_____

_____

_____

_____

_____

_____

What does Romans 11:11–15 reveal about why the gospel has spread to the nations?

_____

_____

_____

_____

_____

_____

_____

How do the following passages illustrate Paul's belief that the gospel is to the Jew first?

- Acts 9:18–20:

_____

_____

_____

_____

_____

_____

_____

- Acts 13:5:

_____

_____

_____

_____

_____

_____

- Acts 13:13–15:

_____

_____

_____

_____

_____

_____

_____

- Acts 14:1:

_____

_____

_____

_____

_____

_____

- Acts 17:1–3:

_____

_____

_____

_____

_____

_____

_____

Dig Deep Into
the Scriptures

Read Matthew 24:14.

What are the Hebrew and Greek translations for the word "nations"?

_____

_____

_____

_____

_____

_____

What is the literal definition of the Greek word for nations?

_____

_____

_____

_____

_____

_____

_____

How does this definition influence your understanding of the call to take the gospel to every nation?

_____

_____

_____

_____

_____

_____

_____

_____

_____

_____

_____

_____

_____

_____

When Jesus said the gospel of the kingdom must be preached to every *ethnos*, He was not saying we had to reach only geopolitical countries. He was saying we had to reach the distinct ethnic groups that live within those countries. When this is coupled with what Paul tells us in Romans 1:16, that the gospel is "to the Jew first" and then to the nations, we see the priority of taking the gospel to every community in every country where the Jewish people have been scattered. This may very well be the missing link in world outreach. Reaching the Jewish people is a vitally important key to reaching the nations for Yeshua.

PAUL'S AMAZING STATEMENT

Paul was called "the apostle to the Gentiles" (Rom. 11:13), yet he said in Romans 9:2–5: "My sorrow is great and the anguish in my heart unending. For I would pray that I myself were cursed, banished from Messiah for the sake of my people—my own flesh and blood, who are Israelites. To them belong the adoption and the glory and the covenants and the giving of the Torah and the Temple service and the promises. To them belong the patriarchs—and from them, according to the flesh, the Messiah, who is over all, God, blessed forever."

List at least two of the four possible reasons Paul said he would be willing to give up his salvation to see his Jewish brethren know their Messiah.

How does Romans 11:11-12 let us know the Jews' rejection of the Messiah is only temporary?

How do we as believers in Yeshua provoke the Jews to jealousy?

How do the following verses prophesy that the Jewish people are to be a light to the nations, to be carriers of God's love, salvation, and redemption?

- Psalm 67:4–6:

_____

_____

_____

_____

_____

_____

- Isaiah 2:2–3:

_____

_____

_____

_____

_____

_____

- Isaiah 42:6–7:

_____

_____

It was only after Yeshua had poured Himself out completely to reach the Jewish people that the doors swung
wide to allow people from every nation to enter God's
kingdom. In the Book of Revelation, John gives this glorious prophecy of people from all over the world praising
God together:

> After these things I looked, and behold, a vast multi-
> tude that no one could count—from every nation and
> all tribes and peoples and tongues—was standing
> before the throne and before the Lamb. They were
> clothed in white robes, with palm branches in their
> hands and crying out with a loud voice, saying,
> "Salvation belongs to our God, who sits on the throne,
> and to the Lamb!"
>
> —REVELATION 7:9–10

Yes, the gospel is still to the Jew first. It is the missing key
of missiology. And when this precedent is followed, it will
release greater openness to the gospel in the nations.

BLESS ISRAEL

Paul begins Romans 10 by saying, "Brothers and sisters, my heart's desire and my prayer to God for Israel is for their salvation."

How are you praying for the salvation of the Jewish people?

_____

_____

_____

_____

_____

_____

If you don't know any Jewish people personally, pray that the Lord brings a Jewish person into your life, and in the meantime pray for Jewish people in general. And if you do have Jewish friends, don't shy away from sharing your faith with them. Of course, be tactful and wait for the right timing. Don't shove the gospel down their throats, but share your testimony with them. Tell them how the God of Israel changed your life. Every believer has a role to play in God's plan for the Jewish people. When they turn their hearts toward Messiah, Israel will be restored, and we will move another major step toward His return.

PRAYER JOURNAL

Use this space to record any insights, scriptures, or answers to prayer you receive as you spend time praying for the peace of Jerusalem and the salvation of the Jewish people.

SESSION FOUR

KEY SIX:
Bringing Life From the Dead

KEY SEVEN:
The Restoration of All Things

Before you begin, read chapters 6 and 7 of
Unlocking the Prophetic Mysteries of Israel.

I N THE PREVIOUS session we discussed that the gospel is to the Jew first. Yet because of their rejection of the gospel, it has been released to the other nations of the world. In this session we will explore what the Jewish people's acceptance of the Messiah releases—"life from the dead"—and then the final key, the restoration of all things.

KEY SIX:
BRINGING LIFE FROM THE DEAD

Because of Israel's rejection of Messiah, the gospel has now gone to the Gentiles, as we discussed in session three. But just as the Israelites' rejection of the gospel brought a particular result, so will their acceptance of the good news. Their rejection released the gospel to go to the other nations of the world, but their acceptance releases something else— "life from the dead" upon the church and the nations.

Again, we see in Romans 11:11–15:

> I say then, they did not stumble so as to fall, did they? May it never be! But by their false step salvation has come to the Gentiles, to provoke Israel to jealousy. Now if their transgression leads to riches for the world, and their loss riches for the Gentiles, then how much more their fullness! But I am speaking to you who are Gentiles. Insofar as I am an emissary to the Gentiles, I spotlight my ministry if somehow

I might provoke to jealousy my own flesh and blood and save some of them. For if their rejection leads to the reconciliation of the world, what will their acceptance be but life from the dead?

This passage lets us know that if we want to see an outpouring of the Spirit on the nations of the world, we must pray for the salvation of Israel. When Israel turns to the Messiah, "life from the dead" will flow into every corner of the globe! This will be the start of the biggest revival in history.

Imagine the soul-winning crusades of Billy Graham multiplied many times over. It will be far greater than all the revivals led by the great evangelists of history—Charles Spurgeon, Dwight L. Moody, Charles Finney, John Wesley, Jonathan Edwards, Billy Sunday, and everyone else you can think of—combined.

It will be the great outpouring spoken of in Joel 3:1: "I will pour out My *Ruach* [Spirit] on all flesh: your sons and daughters will prophesy, your old men will dream dreams, your young men will see visions."

Describe what "life from the dead" would look like if it does indeed refer to finishing the work of atonement that restores the earth to the way it was before the fall of man. What would a world that operates as it was originally intended to—without sickness, pain, death, or suffering of any kind—be like?

_____

_____

_____

_____

_____

_____

_____

It is only when we die to self that the Spirit of God can live within us and make Himself known through us. In what ways do you need to die to self?

_____

_____

_____

_____

_____

_____

How did Yeshua defeat death?

_____

_____

_____

_____

_____

_____

When the veil was torn in two after Yeshua's death, what did it signify? (See Matthew 27:51 and Hebrews 9:1–9.)

_____

_____

_____

_____

_____

_____

What are some signs in both Israel and the Muslim world of a greater openness to the gospel—that the light of Yeshua is shining brighter as the world grows darker?

_____

_____

_____

_____

_____

_____

In the previous session we looked at Romans 9:1–4, where the apostle Paul shares his willingness to give up his own salvation for his unbelieving Jewish brothers. We considered some reasons Paul may have been willing to make such a sacrifice. Perhaps there is another reason that we have not yet explored—the fact that the Israelites' acceptance of their Messiah would bring "life from the dead" to the world and the return of Yeshua to Earth.

Another way of saying it might be, "For I would be willing to give up my own salvation to see God's ultimate plan for the world accomplished." You see, Paul understood that the key to God's plan for the redemption of the world, or "life from the dead," was connected to Israel's salvation, and for that cause Paul was willing to sacrifice even his own salvation.

KEY SEVEN:
THE RESTORATION OF ALL THINGS

If you've ever experienced loss, you know how devastating it can be. That is why "life from the dead" is such an exciting prospect. We have all lost things and people that are important to us. Some of us have lost jobs and investments; others have lost friends to betrayal or spouses to divorce.

Loss is all around us—but it won't always be this way. When the Messianic age comes, God is going to restore to us everything we have lost. And those days of restoration are closer than ever before. The apostle Paul said it best in Romans 8:18–23:

> I consider the sufferings of this present time not worthy to be compared with the coming glory to be revealed to us. For the creation eagerly awaits the

revelation of the sons of God. For the creation was subjected to futility—not willingly but because of the One who subjected it—in hope that the creation itself also will be set free from bondage to decay into the glorious freedom of the children of God. For we know that the whole creation groans together and suffers birth pains until now—and not only creation, but even ourselves. We ourselves, who have the first-fruits of the *Ruach*, groan inwardly as we eagerly wait for adoption—the redemption of our body.

What do the following passages of Scripture reveal about what Earth will be like when all things are restored to the way God meant them to be?

- Isaiah 11:6–10:

_____

_____

_____

_____

_____

_____

- Ezekiel 36:33–35:

_____

_____

_____

_____

_____

_____

_____

When the "restoration of all things" takes place, the world and everything in it will change for the better. Weeds and thistles will be transformed into beautiful flowers and plants. Vicious wild animals will become tame and friendly. No child will be hungry, sick, or alone. In fact, no one will be without nutritious food, robust health, or friendship. Starvation and pollution will cease. Best of all, we will all know fellowship with God similar to the fellowship Adam and Eve had with Him in the garden. God Himself says that during those days, "It will come to pass that before they call, I will answer, and while they are still speaking, I will hear" (Isa. 65:24).

Give some examples from chapter 7 of *Unlocking the Prophetic Mysteries of Israel* of how revivals have corresponded with milestones in Israel's history.

_____

_____

_____

_____

_____

What does it mean to you for the church to come into the fullness of its identity as children of Abraham?

_____

_____

_____

_____

_____

_____

In what ways can Gentile believers seek to better understand the Jewish origins of their faith?

_____

_____

_____

_____

_____

_____

There has been a clear link between the return of the Jewish people to their land and the outpouring of blessing upon the church. It isn't just a coincidence that the Toronto outpouring was characterized by holy laughter and joy. Psalm 126:1–3 says that when the Lord restored the fortunes of Zion, "our mouths were filled with laughter, our tongues with songs of joy. Then it was said among the nations, 'The LORD has done great things for them.' The LORD has done great things for us, and we are filled with joy" (NIV).

DIG DEEP INTO
THE SCRIPTURES

Read Acts 3:11–21 (NIV).

What is the literal translation of the Hebrew word *t'shuva* used in verse 19?

_____

_____

_____

_____

_____

_____

_____

How can we understand salvation in light of this definition?

_____

_____

What is Peter telling the Jewish people in this passage?

What is the phrase "times of refreshing" most commonly interpreted to mean? What does it mean to you?

What else does Peter believe God will send when the Jewish people *t'shuva*?

_____

_____

_____

_____

_____

_____

_____

What is Yeshua doing until the set time for His return?

_____

_____

_____

_____

_____

_____

_____

SIGNS OF THE TIMES

Let's look again at Acts 3:21: "...until the time of the restoration of all the things that God spoke about long ago through the mouth of His holy prophets," or as the NIV says, "...until the time comes for God to restore everything, as he promised long ago through his holy prophets."

What are some signs of "the restoration of all the things" spoken of in Acts 3:21? (See chapter 7 of *Unlocking the Prophetic Mysteries of Israel*, pages 149–150.)

_____

_____

_____

_____

_____

_____

Tribulation will be part of end-times events. What are some reasons mankind will experience tribulation and turmoil in the last days?

_____

_____

_____

_____

_____

_____

_____

_____

_____

Should those who belong to God fear tribulation in the last days? Explain.

_____

_____

_____

_____

_____

_____

_____

Have you ever seen glimpses of the original beauty of creation beneath all the mess and grime caused by sin? If so, describe them.

_____

_____

_____

_____

_____

_____

_____

The Scriptures give dozens of examples of the glorious events that will take place during the coming

Messianic age. List three of the ten hallmarks of the Messianic age cited in chapter 7.

_____

_____

_____

_____

_____

_____

_____

_____

Many people have tried to predict when the Messiah will return; some even gave specific dates. Why do you believe the Messiah will return "like a thief in the night" (1 Thess. 5:2)?

_____

_____

_____

_____

_____

_____

_____

This world is about to change in every possible way. If you're ready, this will be extremely good news for you. As the apostle Paul declared, "Things no eye has seen and no ear has heard, that have not entered the heart of mankind— these things God has prepared for those who love Him" (1 Cor. 2:9).

Stay alert. Keep watching. And above all, don't give up. No matter what you have gone through, or are going through right now, the future will be absolutely magnificent.

BLESS ISRAEL

Before He ascended into heaven, Yeshua told His disciples, "This Good News of the kingdom shall be proclaimed in the whole world as a testimony to all the nations, and then the end will come" (Matt. 24:14). This means the gospel must be preached to every nation on Earth before the Messiah's return. Who shares the good news of God's love and supports efforts to spread it into every nation? We do! To quote the apostle Paul, "How then shall they call on the One in whom they have not trusted? And how shall they trust in the One they have not heard of? And how shall they hear without someone proclaiming?...faith comes from hearing, and hearing by the word of Messiah" (Rom. 10:14, 17).

People are not going to be saved unless they believe, and for that to happen, they first must hear. Who is to tell them? One of the most important ways you can be directly involved in Yeshua's return is by spreading the good news of eternal life by sharing your faith with those around you. When you help take the gospel to Jewish people all over the world so they can hear, believe, and be saved, Romans 11:15 will come to pass, and life will come from the dead.

What do you believe God would have you do to help spread the gospel to the nations and prepare the way for Yeshua's return?

Prayer Journal

Use this space to record any insights, scriptures, or answers to prayer you receive as you spend time praying for the peace of Jerusalem and the salvation of the Jewish people.

_____

_____

_____

_____

_____

_____

_____

_____

_____

_____

_____

_____

_____

_____

_____

_____

_____

_____

_____

_____

_____

_____

NOTES

SESSION ONE

1. Jaroslav Pelikan, *Jesus Through the Centuries* (New Haven, CT: Yale University Press, 1985), 20.

SESSION THREE

1. "History of Jerusalem: Timeline for the History of Jerusalem (4500 BCE–Present)," Jewish Virtual Library, accessed September 5, 2017, http://www.jewishvirtual library.org/timeline-for-the-history-of-jerusalem -4500-bce-present.

2. "Ancient Jewish History: The Bar-Kokhba Revolt (132– 135 CE)," Jewish Virtual Library, accessed September 5, 2017, http://www.jewishvirtuallibrary.org/the-bar-kokhba -revolt-132-135-ce.

3. "Vital Statistics: Jewish Population of the World (1882– Present)," Jewish Virtual Library, accessed September 5, 2017, http://www.jewishvirtuallibrary.org/jewish -population-of-the-world.

ABOUT THE AUTHOR

JONATHAN BERNIS is the president and CEO of Jewish Voice Ministries International and the author of several books, including *A Hope and a Future*, *A Rabbi Looks at Jesus of Nazareth*, *A Rabbi Looks at the Last Days*, *A Rabbi Looks at the Afterlife*, and *A Rabbi Looks at the Supernatural*. Bernis is a Jewish believer in Jesus who has been in Messianic Jewish ministry for over thirty-five years and is the host of *Jewish Voice With Jonathan Bernis*, a weekly television program seen on Christian networks across the globe. Bernis and his wife, Elisangela, are the parents of two daughters, Liel and Hannah, and reside in Phoenix, Arizona.

To learn more about Jewish Voice Ministries International, visit www.jewishvoice.org.